My Awesome Humility

And How I Attained It

#ChoosingPositiveSelfImage

www.MyAwesomeHumility.com

Glen Aubrey

Author, Publisher, Professional Musician,
Emmy ® Award Winner, Consultant

Creative Team Publishing
Fort Worth, Texas

© 2018 by Glen Aubrey.

All rights reserved. No part of this book may be reproduced, stored in a retrieval system or transmitted in any form or by any means without the prior written permission of the publisher, except by a reviewer who may quote brief passages in a review distributed through electronic media, or printed in a newspaper, magazine, or journal.

Disclaimers:
- Due diligence has been exercised to obtain written permission for use of references, quotes, or imagery where required. Any additional quotes, references, or imagery may be subject to the Fair Use Doctrine. Where additional references, quotes, or imagery may require source credit, upon written certification that such a claim is accurate, credit for use will be noted on the book's website, www.MyAwesomeHumility.com.
- The opinions and conclusions expressed are solely those of the author and/or the individuals and entities represented and are limited to the facts, experiences, and circumstances involved. No professional, psychological, or medical advice is implied, stated, or offered in any way whatsoever. You are encouraged to seek professional help, education, advice, and counsel from individuals you deem competent should you desire to learn more about human behavior, character traits, insecurity, self-confidence, or any medically related topic.
- Note that certain names and related circumstances may have been changed to protect confidentiality. All stories where names are mentioned are used with the permission of the parties involved, if applicable. Any resemblance to past or current people, places, circumstances, or events is purely coincidental.

ISBN: 978-0-9979519-5-0

PUBLISHED BY CREATIVE TEAM PUBLISHING
www.CreativeTeamPublishing.com
Ft. Worth, Texas
Printed in the United States of America

Table of Contents

About This Book   7

Introduction: Please Meet the Real You   15

Chapter One:
Standards for Personal Growth   21
    The Code of Achievement   25
    The Four Questions   26

Chapter Two:
The Power of Choosing a Positive Attitude   35
    Fatigue   36
    Keep the Dream Alive   38

Chapter Three:
There Are Some Behaviors You Should Not Tolerate or Permit within Yourself or Others   47
    Behaviors Showcase Truth about Personal Character   49

Table of Contents

Chapter Four:
The Labels You Wear May Not be The Best
Indicators of Who You Really Are   53
    A Personal Creed   57
    Twelve Laws of Understanding   60
    My Personal Creed   62
    Values, Vision, Mission, Message   64

Chapter Five:
A False Sense of Control—Get Over It   67

Chapter Six:
You and Others Can Learn How to Give and
Receive, and Become Exemplary Models of
Gracious Living   73
    Conflict Resolution   75
    Trust   76
    The Value of a Sincere Apology   79
    The Mentors in Your Life   84
    Completing or Competing?   90

Chapter Seven:
Slow Down Enough to Do Something
Beneficial for You   93

Table of Contents

**Chapter Eight:
You Become a Leader When You Care More about Others than Yourself, Because You Are Secure in Who You Are** 99

**Chapter Nine:
Be Well, Love Well, Lead Well, Invest Well, and Feel Good about It** 107

**Chapter Ten:
It's Work and You Are Worth It** 113
    Take Us Home 115
    Rested and Home 118

Closing Thoughts 121

*****

Credits in Order of Appearance 123

Products and Services 127

About the Author 129

*****

About This Book

My Awesome Humility and How I Attained It

This is a book about choosing a positive self-image.

This is a book of confidence, assurance, and true humility. This study represents hard work for you if you choose to embrace what you read.

In these pages you will observe challenging human behaviors and learn why a low or self-effacing self-image is, or can be, detrimental to you and everyone within your network — family, friends, professional associations (at work, for example) — indeed, everyone with whom you have association, including those who influence you and those over whom you exert influence.

You will also see examples of the negative effects of blatant arrogance. Arrogance and self-confidence are absolutely *not* the same. Both are choices.

Arrogance, bullying, and intimidation are often born of severe insecurity. In contrast, self-confidence and assurance, accompanied by authentic humility, emerge from growing personal contentment and a commitment to improve. When you improve, you are in a better position to help others who truly want to grow.

A relevant journey of self-analysis and a choice for self-improvement are not options everyone or perhaps even most people choose to take. In fact, some feel truly threatened by learning their core issues, and may express high trepidation when shown opportunities for positive change. Ultimately, you alone consider advancing your character and changing your behaviors if you agree.

These life lessons, born in truth and conveyed from a desire to achieve maximum positive results, can become part and parcel of your core makeup if you desire, and they rest on a foundation of self-love. Upon that foundation, personal success in its purest form is or can be built.

The more explicit you are in defining what you want for yourself and why, the more prepared you become to achieve what you truly desire, especially if your heart is in the right place, you possess right motives, your actions corroborate your motives, and you act according to higher law.

This book is written for those who are deemed healthy emotionally and intellectually. It offers someone with a desire and capability to grow, strong encouragement to receive input, and solid alternatives to learned, chosen, and practiced defective and self-destructive habits.

This book is written to encourage you to become the best person you can be, patterning your choices after proven and life-giving principles and practices, eternal standards.

My Awesome Humility and How I Attained It

This book is offered to help you truly believe and achieve the ultimate best about you because <u>you are worth it</u>.

Be prepared to wrestle with gut level and vital truths. It can be hard work because it is a meritorious endeavor. The journey takes belief, diligence, and most of all, earnest desire.

The central premise is this: You are a viable and valuable human being. If you agree with that central premise, then it will be up to you to put actions in place that truly can alter who you perceive yourself to be and what you believe you can accomplish.

Here are several salient points in a few short sentences. See how many, if any, merit your investigation and possible agreement.

1. You are a person of great value.

2. You are more important than what you do.

3. What you do is important because of who you are.

4. All you are and what you contribute have immense worth.

5. What you believe about yourself becomes part of defining your character.

6. Your character gives birth to your choice of actions.

7. Your life experiences, good and bad, contribute to how you understand yourself.

8. Learn from your experience and make good choices.

9. Your past mistakes can be forgiven.

10. You can make a new start if you want to.

11. Determine what you want and why you want it.

12. Your desires help determine your attitude and aptitude, and contribute to your choices of action.

Regardless of circumstances, you choose your attitudes and actions. These choices ultimately chart your destiny and impact the people around you.

> Regardless of circumstances, you choose your attitudes and actions.
> These choices ultimately chart your destiny and impact the people around you.

A choice for personal victory replaces perceptions of personal victimization or unworthiness. A choice for conquering fear with love is a God-birthed promise of human interaction that transcends doubt and overcomes the feelings of negative interactions, no matter what they are.

If you are a person of faith you accept the fact that you are a creation of God. That fact alone makes you unique, valuable, special, a treasure.

While this book is not a "religious" book, it does recognize and fully accept the fact that as a created being, you are endowed by your Creator with worth.

The United States Declaration of Independence, authored by Thomas Jefferson, stated it this way (underline emphasis added):

IN CONGRESS, JULY 4, 1776
The unanimous Declaration of the thirteen
united States of America

"When in the Course of human events it becomes necessary for one people to dissolve the political bands which have connected them with another and to assume among the powers of the earth, the separate and equal station to which the Laws of Nature and of Nature's God entitle them, a decent respect to the opinions of mankind requires that they should declare the causes which impel them to the separation.

"<u>We hold these truths to be self-evident, that all men are created equal, that they are endowed by their Creator with certain unalienable Rights, that among these are Life, Liberty and the pursuit of Happiness.</u> — That to secure these rights, Governments are instituted among Men, deriving their just powers from the consent of the governed,…"

The signers of the Declaration made this solemn commitment:

"And for the support of this Declaration, with a firm reliance on the protection of Divine Providence, we mutually pledge to each other our Lives, our Fortunes, and our sacred Honor."
~ From www.ushistory.org/declaration/

While the inherent value of a person can be recognized apart from a belief in God, when value is authored by God, Himself, and affirmed by other human beings because of a person's divine origin, it then becomes a true recognition of a God-shaped piece in every individual, intrinsic in a person's actual makeup.

My Awesome Humility and How I Attained It

You are a creation of God. Because God made you, you have value. Because you possess inherent value it is important to consider yourself for who you really are.

Perhaps you need to be introduced to the real you.

Introduction:

[_____ ,]
(Your Name)

Please Meet the Real You.

Let me ask you to introduce yourself to your true person. Please fill in both lines with your first and last name:

_____ ,

Please Meet the Real Person Who Is Also Known as:

_____ .

Then say, "This person is a treasure and a gift from God. I respect him/her and honor him/her for who he/she is and the good that he/she accomplishes."

Now please, sign your name:

_____

If you made the introduction with sincerity how did meeting the real you really feel? How well do you honestly know the true you? What are the characteristics of the person you truly are? Those are not simple questions with simple answers. They're not designed to be.

Let's not complicate this, however. Bottom line: the characteristics of your inner true self, your core being, must become known to you as much as is possible, especially for a healthy self-image to emerge and be recognized. Without this knowledge it will be difficult to embark on improvement.

Please take a moment and list your positive traits: the characteristics you celebrate or want to celebrate about yourself. (You may benefit from utilizing a Google search of personality and character traits to help you choose the ones you believe best describe you.) Use an additional sheet if necessary.

Go on. Honestly see the real you, the person you are proud of. This is a list of healthy traits ... not a list of boasts. Please list several on each line. Fill up the pages as much as you can. Be sincerely proud of the positive person you are.

_____
_____
_____
_____
_____
_____
_____
_____

My Awesome Humility and How I Attained It

Now please list the traits about yourself you would like to change, to improve the real you. Again, honestly approach this exercise. Are these negative traits? Perhaps ... and yes. They represent opportunities for you to grow in ways you may have never considered.

_____
_____
_____
_____
_____
_____
_____
_____
_____
_____
_____
_____
_____
_____
_____
_____
_____
_____

My Awesome Humility and How I Attained It

_____
_____
_____
_____
_____
_____
_____
_____

Consider what was difficult and what was easy about this exercise. If in fact you took it seriously, how much would you like to alter the negative traits in ways that could transform you? There are some negatives you can fix and likely some you can't. You are probably not able to change everything you would like to, but at least you know what behaviors or characteristics you want to change.

Chapter One

Standards for Personal Growth

"It's hard to be humble when you are as great as I am." How many times have you heard that before? Actually, the opposite is true. Real humility is possible only when a person knows who he or she is, and chooses to be humble for the right reasons. True humility is a choice. When that choice is made, it really cannot be talked about too much or humility vanishes!

> Real humility is possible only when a person knows who he or she is, and chooses to be humble for
> the right reasons. True humility is a choice.

It is subpar when community service organizations or individuals talk about their good deeds and award themselves for their charitable services. It would be better to help others and good causes without talking about it. Recognition emerging from those who talk about all they've done can be misplaced. Bragging can become a motive for self-glorification and "tooting your own horn." It's unnecessary.

The superior option: serve without seeking recognition. When service is recognized, let accolades originate from those receiving the service, not engaging in it.

Don't do good to make others notice you. That is not pure love and true selfless giving. Provide good service because you desire to help and truly do not care about getting credit.

"Love your neighbor as yourself." It's called the second Great Commandment. The first one is a command to love God fully. This second commandment teaches how to relate to others. These commandments are found in the Bible, in the Gospel of Mark, Chapter 12, verses 30 and 31.

Look closely at this one:

> **"Love your neighbor as yourself."**

Most people have heard the injunction, "Love one another." On one level, to love someone means you care enough to sacrifice for their benefit, giving without any expectation of return. True and authentic love is selfless. It emerges from one who loves himself or herself first because that individual is secure in who he or she really is.

My Awesome Humility and How I Attained It

How much do you love yourself? You cannot love another without first loving yourself. You can't give away something you don't have. As you've heard, "You cannot pour from an empty cup." If you don't love yourself, you have little or nothing to give to anyone.

> You cannot love another without first loving yourself.
> You can't give away something you don't have.

"Love yourself" is the first standard for personal growth. Unless you love you, your love for someone else might look and feel shallow because it is.

> "Love yourself" is the first standard for personal growth. Unless you love you, your love for someone else might look and feel shallow because it is.

How do you know you love you? Loving yourself from a position of surety and security is possible, and that's the reason for this book.

By what standards do you weigh the value of your self-love, true identity, contributions, and desires to improve who you really are?

> By what standards do you weigh the value of your self-love, true identity, contributions, and desires to improve who you really are?

Let me offer some recommendations.

No one is an island, we know this. All people are influenced by others and exert some degree of influence over others as well.

We choose how we relate to one another. If we choose to love truly, without selfish intent, there are costs involved. These costs, when paid, are expended for the benefit of others. Loving, most definitely, includes a price tag for the giver, but loving this way is almost always a positive choice.

If we choose not to love, there are expenditures there, too. Over time, it costs far more for one not to love, to harbor hatred, possess unforgiving attitudes, to promote or take revenge, to act destructively toward other people, to lie, cheat, and undercut someone else, to promote and live in ill will, exercise greed, possess and practice racial prejudice, and in general choose to treat others unfairly, inappropriately, unethically, or illegally. One who practices negative deeds because of a desire to hurt another bears the greatest ill will within themselves. Those attitudes, choices, and actions can destroy the bearer.

My Awesome Humility and How I Attained It

Choose well and choose life. How does one know what choices are right? Let me invite you to use the next few minutes to explore a collection of standards against which you can measure personal growth for yourself and others within your network, those with whom you interact on multiple levels.

The book, *Leadership Is – How to Build Your Legacy* presents **The Code of Achievement**, and **The Four Questions.** These standards for personal growth can help you develop your true and desired self.

The Code of Achievement is a vital part of self-love and of any personal investment into other peoples' lives. It is comprised of **Values, Vision, Mission, and Message**.

The Code of Achievement

1. **Values** constitute the core principles upon which agreement exists between a leader and followers and are made up of intangibles that never change.

2. **Vision** describes an overall purpose, the reasons why actions are considered, and the hopes for what the future can be in goal accomplishment. Through vision, cause and motive give meaning to activity.

3. **Mission** is made up of the tasks to complete, the methods used to achieve the goals, the evaluations that show success or failure, and the tangible rewards to be received when the mission is accomplished.

4. **Message** represents life-lessons learned through the fulfillment of the message that impact people with truth. Message is the acquired knowledge that is applied with wisdom.

The Four Questions

The Four Questions compose the foundation to a person's understanding of who they are and how they operate. Answers to these questions may assist a person to know how to function best on their own, or on a team, or in a group. The answers can help a person really know their personal makeup.

1. **Who are you at your core?**
   *This is a question of **values**.* This question seeks to know the heart-core of the individual, what makes them tick, what are their principled, unchangeable, bedrock beliefs upon which their entire world-view and actions are based. These values will likely include, but not be limited to, intangibles of integrity, trust, commitment, faithfulness, respect, cooperation, and love.

2. **What are you called to accomplish?**
   *This is a question of **vision**.* Vision gives purpose. Where this question is answered with a list of tangibles, a person is veering off course. Accomplishments are heart-related when they seek to build up other people and accomplish goals through investment. Vision is best described in intangibles. When someone answering refers to benefits seen in values as opposed to benefits seen in valuables, the question and answer are hitting home.

3. **What do you want?**
   *This is a question of **mission**.* Mission is composed of actions to fulfill a goal. Accomplishment is seen in the effects, both materially and within a frame of mind. What anyone who desires personal growth wants should be in direct correlation to their answers to the first two questions. Mission will include hard work and the satisfaction coming from completing a job well. Happiness should be evidenced in tangible rewards—the products of achievement—along with intangible inner repose—an assurance of attainment, a healthy sense of pride in the fulfillment of purpose.

4. **Whom will you impact?**
   *This is a question of **message**.* Lessons learned are worth little until they become operative in real life. People long for and appreciate authenticity when actions verify words. People who are impacted for

good because of a follower's or leader's life model can find themselves in a state of receptivity for learning what, how, and why something or someone worked. Principled truth that invades and transforms life makes people take notice, and for those who desire more than mediocrity, it creates hunger for more of whatever "that" is and wherever "it" came from. Message is seen through measures and methods. Message is enfolded into desires, decisions, and deeds. The life-lessons learned and taught to those who observe and want to receive them, become the message.

Use these truths as standards of measurement if you agree. Ask yourself, "What traits within or about me do I wish to improve? What characteristics of me would I like to change for the better, and by what methods may I seek to accomplish this change?"

Improvements will probably not happen too quickly, though some may. Speed of behavioral change may not be as rapid as you'd like; some old and negative habits die hard. You may benefit most when you pursue self-improvement in steady, sequential improvements over time. A key is: how much do you want positive change and for what reasons? If it's about improving you so you can positively impact and help others, congratulations. You're on the right track.

My Awesome Humility and How I Attained It

Someone has said, "If you want to love more, love. If you want to help others more, help." But do so without an expectation of return or trumpeting your own contributions. That last part may prove to be the most difficult.

The title of this book is intentional. It is composed of two blatant oxymoron phrases.

My Awesome Humility and How I Attained It

Please note:

1. Humility is not something about which to boast. Arrogance and humility are antithetical.

2. The book's title might be confusing at first, perhaps it helped you smile, or caused you concern.

3. One thing is certain: as you grow to love you, and as you choose humility because you desire to serve others from a position of personal strength and security, then you won't care who gets the credit. You'll just do it.

4. That choice of perspective may become part of a life altering, personal behavioral change!

> One thing is certain: as you grow to love you, and as you choose humility because you desire to serve others from a position of personal strength and security, then you won't care who gets the credit. You'll just do it.

You might wish to seek professional guidance to help you with this growing process. One size of help and encouragement definitely does not fit all. Perhaps trusted clergy, counselors, and friends can assist. Consider that you'll want to choose your counselors and advice givers carefully. Seek multiple opinions and input from people you trust as you chart your course for change.

Above all, look squarely at your motives and understand why you want to become a better person. The reasons will be first for *you* (love yourself) and *then for others* (love your neighbor *as* you love yourself). This order cannot be altered if true and lasting personal growth is desired.

A journey of personal growth which includes positive behavioral change may seem daunting, but it doesn't have to be. It can be fun, too, as well as meaningful. "Fun and meaningful" works for me.

One method I've employed for personal development is positive self-talk. Yes, really. When I was in high school I was part of a winning forensic speech team. We were well-respected because we won tournament after tournament locally, state championships often, and in two cases, international championships. Rehearsals for tournaments often meant hours and hours of personal memorization efforts and a lot of "talking to yourself" as we prepared.

Self-talk: Imagine an audience, your audience. You are rehearsing as though this listening group was actually present in the room. (Often times a mirror helps provide a true glimpse of what an audience would see). In your mind you witness your audience's reactions as you go along. How effective are you in communicating to your imaginary audience?

On local tournament days, usually held at a college or university facility, it was often more than a little entertaining or down right comical to see contestants walking and talking to themselves, preparing, gesturing, communicating to thin air where an imaginary audience was paying rapt attention!

Engaging in self-talk about you and who you are or desire to be, and what you want to communicate, can be greatly beneficial. Rehearsing a conversation that hasn't even happened yet, but you know how it could go, helps you prepare. Preparation, affirmation, and expressing out loud the desire for a good outcome, are what self-talk can be all about. Plus, it can be fun and exhilarating!

Be careful who observes and hears you, however. It can look and feel a little weird to others who may not readily understand what you are doing!

Another action I've encouraged many people to take, especially when they have accomplished something positive, is this: "Go to the nearest mirror and say one or more of the following:"

1. "You're good."

2. "You're a gift of God."

3. "You're worth it."

4. "You are choosing a positive outlook today."

Invariably when I tell people they should consider doing this, I hear these responses (often chuckling as they say them):

1. "Okay, thanks. I think I will."

2. "You are so kind. Thank you!"

3. "Wow ... I've never thought of that."

4. "Really? I'll do it! ... especially on Monday mornings!"

My Awesome Humility and How I Attained It

Self-talk can help you promote what you want to believe about you instead of wallowing in misperceptions of negativity or allowing yourself to degrade you.

You may want to try the mirror exercise. You'll feel better (I'll bet).

Of course, you realize that there are some difficulties that absolutely cannot be solved with positive self-talk. And that's not the point. Self-talk, within reason, can help you feel better and stronger about yourself, assist you in your preparation, and build your confidence. Smile when you do it, too. It can work.

> Self-talk can help you promote what you want to believe about you instead of wallowing in misperceptions of negativity or allowing yourself to degrade you.

How ready are you for personal growth? When will you begin and how will you know? How will those around you know?

Chapter Two

The Power of Choosing a Positive Attitude

I've seen this banner occasionally: "Wine a little. You'll feel better." Let's rephrase it: "Win in your attitude. You'll become better." Wine notwithstanding, what do whining and winning mean to you?

A change of attitude, from whining to winning, can be a key to creating and living in a more positive environment, one *you* create. You must do this for yourself; no one else can.

> A change of attitude, from whining to winning,
> can be a key to creating and living in a more positive
> environment, one *you* create.
> You must do this for yourself; no one else can.

Attitude is a choice. You choose a mental frame of mind that is often expressed outwardly through personality, temperament, gestures, voice, and deeds as you confront and deal with circumstances, good or bad.

When my day is long, frustrating, or pressed, I will often intentionally recall that I choose how I deal with difficult circumstances. I choose well when I seek to win and desire to encourage others likewise.

> I choose well when I seek to win and desire to encourage others likewise.

Fatigue

Fatigue can become an insidious and subversive personal enemy. It seeks to repress positive attitudes if allowed to control or overly influence emotions. If you're tired, rest. It's part of balance. Know when to stop working or worrying so you can be rested and at home with who you are and what you are doing.

> Know when to stop working or worrying so you can be rested and at home with who you are
> and what you are doing.

We are encouraged to not become weary in well doing. How about a Bible verse to back that up? Underline emphasis added:

My Awesome Humility and How I Attained It

"Let us not become weary in doing good, for at the proper time <u>we will reap a harvest if we do not give up</u>."
~ Galatians 6:9 (NIV)

Giving up is not an option if a purpose is true and the choice is firm to obtain the fulfillment of a worthy goal.

In 2009 I composed, copyrighted, and published a song called, "Keep the Dream Alive." The song expresses well, for me anyway, how important it is to stay the course when it's the right course for the right reasons. The message is: "Be determined and don't give up!"

The lyrics, followed by the music, are presented on the next few pages.

Glen Aubrey

Keep the Dream Alive
© 2009 Glen Aubrey. All Rights Reserved.

Keep the dream alive
In your heart, in your soul,
Don't give up on the prize,
Keep your eyes on the goal.

When the journey is true,
Then it's all up to you
To pursue, carry on,
It's your life.

Keep the dream alive,
Walk the road you must choose,
With your faith as your guide
Run the race, win or lose.

When the journey is true,
God will bless it for you.
It's your dream, it's your cause,
It's your life.

Challenges come,
Tears multiply,
But with love on your side
You'll continue to try.

My Awesome Humility and How I Attained It

Keep the dream alive,
Overcome any fear.
Standing strong, face the wrong,
Never quit, persevere.

When the journey is true,
Then it's all up to you
To pursue, carry on,
It's your life.

Some say, "You can't,"
Others, "You could."
You'll achieve what you must
'Cause you know that you should.

Keep the dream alive
In your heart, in your soul,
Don't give up on the prize,
Keep your eyes on the goal.

When the journey is true,
Then it's all up to you
To pursue, carry on,
It's your life.

*****

Glen Aubrey

Keep the Dream Alive

Words and Music by Glen Aubrey

Copyright © 2009 Glen Aubrey.
All Rights Reserved. Printed in U.S.A.

My Awesome Humility and How I Attained It

Keep the Dream Alive — 2

41

Glen Aubrey

*****

Larry Wolf is a retired Los Angeles County Sheriff, the Department Chair of Criminal Justice, University of Antelope Valley, Lancaster, California, a book author, music composer, and lyricist. Plus, he is a great friend. I've been privileged to know Larry for 30 years or more.

His most recent book is entitled *Policing Peace – What America Can Do Now To Avoid Future Tragedies*. It's a brilliant piece of work. Order it through www.policingpeace.com. It is published by Creative Team Publishing, © 2017 by Larry Wolf.

Larry quotes Sir Winston Churchill from a speech delivered to the House of Commons on June 4, 1940. The speech is in the Public Domain.

From *Policing Peace:*

> Sir Winston Churchill was known as a back bencher and thought to be an over-the-hill politician with out of date, dangerous ideas. His great cause, the thing that propelled him back into national prominence, was his conviction that Adolph Hitler was evil and should be resisted at all costs.

My Awesome Humility and How I Attained It

As you know when World War II started, Europe was overrun by the Nazis. They had taken over Austria and Czechoslovakia. They invaded Poland, Norway, Denmark, Belgium, the Netherlands, and then France. Only the small vulnerable island of England stood between Hitler and complete domination of Europe.

With the fate of democracy in Europe hanging in the balance, Churchill inspired England to stand alone. Listen to his words:

*"We shall prove ourselves once again to defend our island home, to ride out the storm of war, and to outlive the menace of tyranny, **if necessary for years, if necessary <u>alone</u>.**"*

As Germany prepared to invade Great Britain, many were resigned to the inevitable Nazi victory. This was before Pearl Harbor, before America had entered the war. While many called upon Britain to sue for peace, Churchill would have none of it. He inspired Great Britain to stand up to Hitler and to fight alone. Listen to his words as he prepared his countrymen for the coming air war with the Nazis:

"*Let us therefore brace ourselves to our duties and so bear ourselves that, if the British Empire and its Commonwealth last for a thousand years, men will still say, 'This was their finest hour.'*"

Germany soon attacked from the sky. Night after night the Germans bombed radar stations, air fields, and finally London and civilian targets. And while Britain stood alone, as the bombs fell on London, the whole world was watching ... and many were inspired to fight alongside the British.

Sometimes when you stand alone, others will join you. Eleven American pilots flew alongside British airman during the Battle of Britain, to help save Democracy in Europe. They handed the Germans their <u>first</u> defeat of the war, showing the world that the Nazi war machine wasn't invincible. And when Hitler realized he could not bully Great Britain into submission, he decided to invade Russia ... his fatal mistake and history was changed forever.

It was truly Britain's **finest hour** and Churchill inspired it by standing alone. (underline and bold emphasis added)

My Awesome Humility and How I Attained It

When your day is clouded by circumstances and the sun seems like it is refusing to shine, I am convinced that it will return on another day, at full strength. History teaches this. Count on it.

Your attitude is your choice. Many times when I am taking a flight and have to arrive very early at an airport counter, I answer the "How are you today?" question with these words, smiling and making eye contact: "How do I look?" Regardless of the rejoinder, my response often is, "Well, it's early, but my attitude is great!" It's great because I choose to make it great. That comment almost always causes the people at check-in or the TSA folks to smile.

Discovering the true you and loving who you are, is worth the effort for most. The real you is a precious gift. It is a vital piece of your life to enjoy, to build, and to grow. How you treat this life by your chosen attitude is a choice you make.

> The real you is a precious gift. It is a vital piece of your life to enjoy, to build, and to grow.

How important is it to adopt a positive attitude and uplifting perspective about improving you? There are no greater steps than ones which show that you are valuable enough to build a positive and contributory character and to choose a strong and positive attitude to encourage you and those you encounter.

Glen Aubrey

If you are person of Biblical faith, you likely already know the sentences below are true. If and since these are true, they are right. They'll change you if you believe them and act upon them within that secure belief.

*****

You are God's creation.

God loves you.

God loves you because you are His creation.

God sacrificed for you because He loves you.

Does His sacrifice not prove your worth?

*****

Chapter Three

There are Some Behaviors You Should Not Tolerate or Permit within Yourself or Others

> Behaviors you should not tolerate or permit within yourself or others include bullying, intimidation, destructive criticism (observed in speaking or hearing truth within a negative environment where criticism seeks to demean or diminish your person, character, or positive contributions), blatantly false accusations, lies, putdowns, destructive innuendo, negative talk, fear, recrimination, and veiled or obvious threats ... to mention some.

Our consulting firm, Creative Team Resources Group, CTRG, is rarely called upon to serve a healthy organization. The usual reason we are contacted is because an organization is suffering in its working relationships, functions, and operational structures, regardless of degree.

We have seen many deviant and destructive behaviors along with others that are truly meritorious and positive. The latter is preferred, of course, and becomes the beneficial result for which we work.

See how much you identify with this brief, true story: The first meeting of the large firm began ostensibly enough: honest, good intentions and statements on our parts, and apparent positive attitudes on the parts of the client's leaders and executive staff. Numbering about ten people total in the conference room, including two from CTRG, we began our collective time positively and pleasantly, employing true affirmations, goal setting, and procedure descriptions, describing realistic expectations.

Very quickly, however, certain telltale destructive attitudes, comments, and behaviors emerged from a primary leader of the client's organization and the environment of the meeting went downhill fast. The tactics this so-called leader publicly and audaciously employed were simple and obvious: he tried to intimidate his staff, the consulting firm, and other leaders in the room, clumsily utilizing innuendo, putdowns, false accusations, and destructive criticism.

Our leadership took that for about a minute and faced his negativity head-on. With this rejoinder, directed in no uncertain terms toward this organization's leader, CTRG stated firmly but respectfully: "*YOU* will not intimidate us."

Immediate and awkward silence.

I suppose he could have fired our firm, but didn't. I surmise he reasoned there was too much at stake at that moment in front of us and the others of his firm, and all of us knew it, and he knew we all knew it. This dismal display of grossly ineffective and highly disrespectful leadership had blatantly revealed this needy leader to be nothing more than a bully, highly insecure (more on that in a moment), vicious, and ineffective, far out of touch with his own people. He let the situation ride for a short time — maybe a minute — until another demonstration of his true character emerged: without a word, he abruptly rose from his chair, exited the meeting, and never came back.

How often have you experienced these kinds of gutter behaviors from people in authority over you, or in positions of power and influence? How have you handled them? These kinds of demonstrations of less than adequate leadership are far too prevalent, unfortunately, in today's work and personal environments.

Behaviors Showcase the Truth about Personal Character

Character is on display virtually all the time. It is observed through behaviors.

When deviant behavior dominates, its demonstration is often a sure sign of varying degrees of insecurity. Bullying and intimidation are examples of chosen behaviors that can mask gross feelings of inadequacy. This destitution may reveal itself in an individual who appears to genuinely not love themselves, and who is not strong within their person to interact with others apart from dishing out destructiveness. How much does this individual possess disregard or dislike for him or herself?

If you or someone you know believes they are insecure, regardless of the cause, be on the lookout for behaviors that may seek to put others down in efforts to elevate themselves because they may not consider themselves to be valuable unless they dominate others.

Resorting to behaviors that are far less than encouraging, void of positive interaction, or absent true efforts to engage positively, are evidences of character weakness, pure and simple.

"The meek shall inherit the earth." You've heard that, I am sure. Please hear this: meekness is not weakness. In fact, just the opposite is true. Meekness is powerful. Meekness is controlled strength.

With CTRG we often work with teams of highly qualified building construction leaders. In our interactions we often observe high degrees of leadership weakness when leaders choose less than acceptable behaviors in their interactions with others who work for or with them. These weak leaders demonstrate that they're not strong enough to let others see their true characters, probably fearing that if someone saw who they really were, this revelation would hit them too hard—they couldn't take it. Therefore, they fear the truth and seek to cover their inner, inadequate character with behaviors designed to put others down to build themselves up. They seek to create or discover multiple excuses to behave in this kind of dishonesty.

In one example, I met with a bold and outwardly strong leader one-on-one, and asked him to allow me to shut his office door while we spoke openly and honestly. It took courage and a submitted attitude for him to agree, and he did. We spoke of his obvious strength and discussed what true and resilient leadership really consisted of. Following our talk, he had some choices to make.

In his office, his oversized desk faced a large whiteboard suspended on an opposite wall. On the top of it I wrote "Controlled Strength" as our meeting concluded. I reminded him that just because he *could* do something, empowered by title, position, money, or authority, did not mean that he *should* do it ... and that he was in charge of how he used his strength.

Months went by and I had occasion to visit his office location again. He was not in on the day I arrived and I wasn't expected. I asked the receptionist/security personnel if his office might be open, and would I be permitted to see it, and could an officer accompany me to see it if it was open. The answer was yes. We walked the hallway and found his office. Nothing appeared changed: same desk, furnishings, layout, etc. Upon the large wall opposite his desk, his large whiteboard was prominent. On the top of the whiteboard my message to him, written many months before, was still there ... yes, he had kept it so he could remember.

It takes a person of valiant character to control his or her strength. Controlling strength is not masking or burying it; rather, it is utilizing power in the right ways at right times to affect positive changes when needed and desired to occur.

How strong are you? How insecure? What are the means you employ to deal with those around you, who work for you, over whom you have influence or impact, authority or responsibility? Do you demean and demand, or invest and train?

Where insecurity is present, negative behaviors are often exercised. Who stops this dysfunction and replaces it with better activity? Answer: the person who becomes convinced that humble strength is far superior to dishonest and disheartened weakness.

Choose meekness. Your inheritance may be larger than you think.

Chapter Four

The Labels You Wear May Not be The Best Indicators of Who You Really Are

Her name is Taylor. I have been quite impressed with this young working lady's true assessment of herself. She's strong, pleasant, humble, and thorough. She's a leader, runs a quality enterprise, and commands respect, not because she demands it; rather, because she demonstrates high moral character, quality of provision, hard work, commitment to excellence, and superior service to her staff and customers.

She runs a coffee service place ... and at most times of the day, there isn't too much room available inside ... it's packed with customers, friends, associates. The eats are great, too!

This young lady is also a millennial, by her own admission. She volunteered this once when we were talking about her strong work ethic and her aversion to the expectations of people's participation in "entitlement" which she believed far too many of her generation practiced.

I visit her establishment often ... I am most assuredly a returning customer. I respect her on many levels. And the coffee is fantastic!

As I've pondered her comments more, I've asked her and others of her age: "How much does your generational label really illustrate who you are?" Most of the time the answer I hear includes these words: "Not much." How true.

Labels can be deceptive, if not destructive. If your "label" carries with it character flaws which do not demonstrate who you are, change the label, discard it, or redefine it for you.

What we believe and speak about ourselves and others often places great weight on how we and other people act, react, live up to, or disagree with a label's inherent descriptions. The more we declare what we want in ourselves and in others, using positive and encouraging language, the more we grow opportunities to build uplifting and contributory character.

People, regardless of age, who genuinely feel or demand entitlement from family, government, or other so-called "benefactors", may be living in a false reality, though it appears to be reality to them. Bottom line: No one *owes* anyone anything in the final analysis.

My Awesome Humility and How I Attained It

That isn't to say that people who truly need help should not receive it. Charity is a welcome delight both to exercise and receive when motives, methods, and means are right. We are not speaking of granting and participating in charity here, however. We are weighing a cultural belief and practice of entitlement which so many think, regardless of age, is how society works or should work. In some cultures perhaps that's the norm.

But there is no excuse for someone who milks a system, who wants to literally steal from others no matter who they are, in efforts to benefit their own positions or lifestyles, and who refuse true ownership of responsibility to provide for themselves.

Laws are established to place limits on behavior. People who steal because they feel "entitled" are breaking the law, plain and simple. People who choose to not follow law often pay negative consequences. People who choose to obey law participate in consequences, too. What kinds of consequences do you want? The consequences a person considers may contribute to their choice of action. It should.

It's a tough but right saying from the Bible in The New Testament, II Thessalonians 3:10 (NIV): [10]For even when we were with you, we gave you this rule: "The one who is unwilling to work shall not eat."

Note the word, "unwilling." Being unwilling to work and still demand of others may be best described as slothful laziness, and where violation of law occurs, is clearly wrong.

Governments who enable those who can work to not work by giving away something not earned, do their populace who receive these handouts no favors; rather, a great disservice. On any level, governments that exercise this kind of provision can decrease the desire for people to want to earn for themselves. Some people, who have suffered greatly, regardless of cause, may need and request more of a hand up than a handout. Give them the motivation to improve and eventually their self-confidence will likely increase and healthy and dignified pride will take the place of selfishness and irresponsibility.

Again, no one is "entitled" to anything. To demand freebies because one is "unwilling" to labor, showcases behaviors born of misaligned priorities and shirks appropriate ownership of duty.

Entitlement is the opposite of true responsibility. My role is to provide for me and my family and others of my network to the degree of my capabilities and desires because of my belief that responsible provision is part of my core character and duty.

Clearly some may try to take advantage of another's actions of responsibility. No matter; provide to the degree you can and should, anyway. Do what you do because it is right.

Many of us have been on both the giving and receiving sides of generosity and provision. We've been able to be generous and joyfully give; at other times we have been the recipients of someone else's generosity. We express heartfelt gratitude and we should.

Where rubber meets road is where an individual, in his or her heart of hearts, chooses to try and keep trying, to own rightful, personal responsibility, so he or she can provide to the highest capability possible and not try to scam a system, lie, cheat, steal, or blame others for a current status, good or bad. No blame is necessary, usually; it may do no good at all.

What is needed is strength of character, solid effort, and a commitment to not give up on a cause in which you believe and is worthy of you.

A Personal Creed

Your character may require regular and continuing developmental guidance and calls to remembrance of what is right, true, and good. The Ten Commandments are not the Ten Suggestions and they are given as a mandate to all and as a code to obey. Following them, or not, is a choice everyone makes.

Many people call lists of collected personal responsibility actions a creed. Committing to a creed can be powerful if that creed is firmly rooted in right and lasting principles.

Upon what do you base your beliefs? If you have not developed a personal creed or a belief system based on lasting truths, it's time. What do you believe about yourself and how do you know what you believe is anchored in truth?

Who or what has contributed to how you act, what you believe, whom you trust, and the truths you espouse? People make changes in action when belief and character change first. Desire is the key. What behaviors do you want to improve because you know these changes are or would be right?

"The results of behavioral changes that are made from desires to improve versus forced improvements (usually policy-dictated) are remarkable. Put another way: people are stronger when they change because they want to, not because they have to. Desire is always preferable to dictate, and choices precede results…"
~ From the book, *Lincoln – The Making of a Leader* by Glen Aubrey, Copyright © 2017, Creative Team Publishing

My Awesome Humility and How I Attained It

> "... people are stronger when they change because they want to, not because they have to. Desire is always preferable to dictate, and choices precede results..."

What does your personal creed include? What do you want it to include? Weighing **The Code of Achievement** and answering **The Four Questions** may help you see what traits about you are those you may desire to change for the better. To become a truer and more desired person is your call, your responsibility, and your opportunity.

> To become a truer and more desired person is your call, your responsibility, and your opportunity.

Several years ago I took the step to compose my personal creed. I titled it, **The Twelve Laws of Understanding**. A business associate jokingly asked, "Understanding what?" I answered, "You. This is for you to understand your core principles."

How well to you understand you, your core beliefs, your essential character traits, and the principles upon which your actions are chosen?

How much do these core truths about you contribute to forming your life creed?

Glen Aubrey

Twelve Laws of Understanding

Copyright © 2004 Glen Aubrey, www.ctrg.com.
From *Leadership Is – How to Build Your Legacy*

1. Realize I am responsible for my own choices, not other's; that changing someone else's behavior is not my responsibility; rather, I need to change me.

2. Seek to understand how the other person thinks and communicates; use his or her language.

3. Model what I want.

4. Set realistic limits on what is acceptable behavior.

5. Impose these limits on myself, first.

6. Desire the best, but prepare for difficulty; seek creative, peaceful solutions.

7. Seek and pray for wisdom.

8. Remember, at the right times.

9. Encourage always.

10. Think first, listen most, and speak seldom.

11. Realize growth involves change, change can mean pain, and patience on the journey is a virtue.

12. Love. Establish meaningful relationships.

My Awesome Humility and How I Attained It

You are invited to <u>compose your Personal Creed</u>. Take the necessary time to think it through thoroughly, and then the needed time to write it down.

Lengthy may not be nearly as important as consistent and accurate. Express what you want, not what you don't want.

See how much of a true alignment exists between your desires to improve and the fundamental and lasting truths upon which morality and law are formed and followed. This personal creed is for you.

Share it with others if you want, those you trust and who truly want your best. Try it.

Write it here if you like. Your composition can make up important steps toward the development, renewal, or beginning of a Personal Creed for you.

Glen Aubrey

My Personal Creed

My Awesome Humility and How I Attained It

_____
_____
_____
_____
_____
_____
_____
_____
_____
_____
_____
_____
_____
_____
_____
_____
_____
_____

Let me share the Code of Achievement: the Values, Vision, Mission, and Message of our organization, Creative Team Resources Group. Our company's creed reflects who we are and what we do. It defines our ethics and standards of operation and reflects our character choices.

Values:

1. Integrity: Truth in word and deed

2. Authenticity: Words and deeds that match

3. Relationships: Decisions about another's success

4. Functional Excellence: Proofs of our relationships

5. Modeling: Duplication into other's lives

6. Legacy: Greater works from our followers

7. Accountability: Completion and closure

8. Enjoyment: Celebration of people and process

9. Rewards: Intangible and tangible results of our efforts

10. Experience: Full engagement on the journey of growth

Vision:

To see lives and organizations changed for the better.

Mission:

We provide great information that encourages people to make better decisions about how they live and work, and we do this through building Core Teams.

Message:

People are more important than what they do. Relationship (the decision about another's success) comes before and gives definition to function.

*****

Why a personal creed? A personal creed offers remembrance and guidance. Visit your creed often. Live it.

Let your personal creed give inspiration and focus to you, your company, or work group. Your creed may serve you well when it represents the values, vision, mission, and message of you the individual, you the participant on a team, or you the leader of an enterprise.

Chapter Five

A False Sense of Control—Get Over It

The difficult issues we confront in organizations, regardless of size, can include patterns of self-absorbed, damaging quests for power and control. This is the condition where greedy individuals take advantage of others to their own and other's detriment, where actions are designed to subvert an organization, its mission, or teams. Unchecked, selfish activities are enemies of building effective and long-lasting legacies. Selfishness thwarts desires to serve in these environments, and individual growth can be stunted.

Where a thirst for power and control at another's expense is prominent, greed rules, and individuals and organizations suffer. Why? Because a quest for control is a fruitless, fake, and false endeavor, one that does not benefit the seeker or anyone else. Get over this false sense of control.

A balance must exist between wanting to succeed and unhealthy control. Truly secure people know how to control themselves to accomplish good and worthy goals personally and professionally. Conversely, misguided endeavors for power and control mask negligence and insecurity, and hinder opportunities to develop healthy characters within their own core makeup. A person who wants to control others to make themselves feel more important is often seen as a self-assuming and arrogant individual, caring very little for anyone else. This person also doesn't regard the damaging effects he or she may have upon others.

> Truly secure people know how to control themselves
> to accomplish good and worthy goals
> personally and professionally.

A person who dwells in greed likely does not or cannot know the full beauty of security, rest, positive engagements in peaceful harmony, and gentle humility. That person may truly miss genuine friendships, love, and cooperation. That person does not appreciate people, and may sacrifice support from those closest to him or her. Then that person wonders why no one wants to be near them except to share power or to be close to it. They may be exceedingly lonely because true and lasting friendships become rare.

A person like this definitely is not living up to their potential and discourages others, too, from seeing theirs. A selfish person may not even know what true potential is. On at least one level, real potential is hidden by greed, and critical, negative viewpoints. This insecure individual relinquishes relationships while severely criticizing and condemning other people. Loneliness abounds.

My Awesome Humility and How I Attained It

> A selfish person may not even know
> what true potential is.

Truly living up to one's potential becomes evidenced more in how much a person possesses and desires to give away, either tangibly or intangibly, or both, than in what he or she strives to control, retain, fearfully hoard, or hide and protect for selfish reasons.

Desiring to control others for one's own benefit is the opposite of thankfulness and giving. Striving for control is a birthplace of greed and possesses a subversive attitude of taking. A person of power and control may care for no one but self. He or she gives nothing because they have nothing to give.

> Desiring to control others for one's own benefit is the
> opposite of thankfulness and giving.

Crime, at its core, is composed of actions that evidence desires to control and manipulate and then seek to hide from the reality of the misdeeds and the negative consequences. Criminals take unlawful advantage of persons or situations in their self-absorption; they try to work a system to their own benefit, often by stealing, murdering, cheating, lying, manipulating, and destroying. People who commit crimes regardless of degree often show little or no regard for the dignity and worth of another person or their property. It's all about them.

People with this misguided behavior may try to justify their actions by claiming victimization—that someone or something "caused" them to act the way they did, that they have become the victims, bearing little or no responsibility for their own condition. Victimization screams a lack of personal responsibility in many cases, and more often than not, blames others for inappropriate or illegal choices. Bottom line: these people believe and live a lie.

Unchecked control and misplaced power may appear to temporarily benefit no one but the power-grabbers. These individuals refuse to take moral and personal responsibility, engaging instead in hatred, falsity, blame, and misguided activity.

> Unchecked control and misplaced power may appear to temporarily benefit no one but the power-grabbers.

Prisons set limits on behaviors by denying freedoms no longer enjoyed because of crimes and convictions. Violations on the outside come with consequences on the inside.

Yes, there are people who have been wrongly convicted. Justice is not always served even though the system of justice in the United States was designed to seek truth and mete out appropriate and correct conclusions. We are not

My Awesome Humility and How I Attained It

focusing on wrong convictions here, however. We are centering on people who, because they have desired control and power to excess, have violated law or other people in their quests to acquire control and power.

You've heard that freedom isn't free. Wars tell us this truth repeatedly. People sacrifice to defend and preserve freedom, but this freedom most assuredly comes with a price. It is also costly when so-called freedoms take unwholesome advantage of others, or when laws are broken. Freedom then is not granted in the same portion, and that which was bought with a price may be not purchased at any price.

Many things we cannot control. We can, however, control us: our attitudes, actions, responses. When we seek control of what we cannot or should not control, temptations toward selfishness take the place of humility, and the ugliness of false power and supremacy rears its head. A wrongful quest for power and control, and the violation or ruin of another as a goal, ultimately hurts the one who desires these subversive dominions.

> Many things we cannot control. We can, however, control us: our attitudes, actions, responses.

Let's choose better. Replace a misguided desire for power and control over others with the discipline to control yourself.

Controlling self is primary and should be a central focus. You and I should control what is given to us — we all possess a responsibility to choose. All of us make choices of attitude and behavior.

> Replace a misguided desire for power and control over others with the discipline to control yourself.

Over what or whom do you feel the need or desire to control? Relationships, other people's actions, how other people feel about you, yours or other people's present courses or future endeavors?

Learning how to relinquish inappropriate control is a lifelong and continual journey. Be refreshed in letting go. Extend grace to others, don't try to control them. Control you.

Chapter Six

You and Others Can Learn How to Give and Receive, and Become Exemplary Models of Gracious Living

Giving and receiving are parts of the same transaction. One is not complete without the other. In the same way, joy and heartfelt thankfulness are parts of the same package, too.

Love is the driving force behind wanting to give, learning to graciously receive, experiencing joy, and choosing to be thankful.

> Love is the driving force behind wanting to give, learning to graciously receive, experiencing joy, and choosing to be thankful.

We are told that love and fear cannot inhabit the same place at the same time. One sure way to know if love is genuine is to ascertain whether fear is part of the mix. If fear is present, rethink and re-do love. Because love is selfless, it doesn't care who gets the credit and refuses to cast blame. And it gets rid of fear.

We are all models for each other. The question never is whether or not you and I are examples to each other; the question always is: what kinds of examples are we? If we choose to be examples of meritorious behavior, we choose well. Driven by love, behaviors seek to help, not hinder.

Have you ever tried pushing water uphill with your bare hands? It's a fruitless activity. In the same way, you cannot help someone who does not desire help.

> You cannot help someone who does not desire help.

But for those who do desire help, your help, do what you can when you can to assist without owning their responsibilities. Let love drive you and become your motivation.

The temptation for power and control can appear when assistance becomes its own goal and control is preferred over investment. In these instances, love is not present.

One of the greatest gifts one can give another is knowledge of how to own solutions and the encouragement to work for them, regardless of who may or may not be watching. Again, this action is driven by selfless love.

Conflict Resolution

One way you and I can learn about gracious living, a part of becoming more secure and confident, is to focus on solving problems, not continuing in conflict. Resolving conflict, confronting problems with a goal of relational and functional rebirth or renewal may not be as difficult as one might think.

In consulting we often are asked to be problem solvers for and with our clients. Our procedures are designed to bring opposing parties together for the purpose of creating a positive environment in which productive conversations can occur, where agreements can be formed, and productive actions commenced. These are also environments of celebration when solutions are implemented and victories are won.

We begin by stating, "We have knowledge of what currently divides you. We understand that disagreements are prevalent, and we respect your opinions. Now, let us ask you a question: 'Upon what do you agree?'"

Sometimes the initial responses are, "Nothing." To which we respond, "Really? You literally agree on nothing? How about the sun coming up tomorrow ... can we agree on that?" Further, "In the case of your positions and responsibilities, what is your mission? To what degree can we agree on that?"

Here's the point: start with ideas or truths upon which agreement exists. Don't try to resolve issues in those areas where agreement does not exist. Start at 30,000 feet with a global view; do not wallow in the weeds of continual conflict. Agreements provide a stronger foundation for producing cooperative, positive, and long-lasting results.

> Start with ideas or truths upon which agreement exists. Don't try to resolve issues in those areas where agreement does not exist.

Trust

Part of developing positive self-image is engaging in trust. We desire this character trait to be active within us and those around us. No requirement in personal or professional relationships is higher in importance than trust.

> No requirement in personal or professional relationships is higher in importance than trust.

There are several kinds or levels of trust. Let me share three and see if these descriptions resonate with you.

The first comes from the knowledge that trust is granted before it is earned. Every relationship, personal, professional, or one of friendship and networking, begins with trust that is not earned. It's often seen in simple courtesy, being polite, exercising kindness and forbearance. Nothing defines initial courtesy more than exercising unearned trust.

> Every relationship, personal, professional, or one of friendship, begins with trust that is not earned.

The second kind of trust is proven or validated trust: One concludes: "I can trust you more because I did it once before and you did not fail; you upheld your part." How refreshing this can be.

With whom do you experience validated trust? Who trusts you because they know they can?

> Who trusts you because they know they can?

Trust is proven over time after a party does what is promised, fulfilling or more than fulfilling requirements or agreements. This kind of trust is seen in commitments that stand and upon which people grow confidence and assurance.

Trust can also be disproven over time and in situations like that, it may become hard or seem impossible to trust the same person or those people again.

Likely we can all relate stories that prove this. How many details can you recall of situations where you trusted and were violated? How many times have you violated someone else's trust?

The courts are filled with people who experience violated trust and who seek justice, compensation, or revenge. Those who violate trust can do great damage, and that damage often brings consequences that endure over many months or years.

Violated trust usually involves at least two individuals or groups: the one who was violated and the one who was the violator. Whether intentional or inadvertent, violated trust places marks on any relationship. These marks, if forgiven, need not remain characteristics of future engagements. The beauty of forgiveness is that past errors don't need to be retained against another person or group if the parties desire wholesome forgiveness and are eager to try again.

It's true: when trust is violated, the trust covenant is severed but it need not remain severed forever. The question of what kind of new or restored relationship is desired comes into play. What is possible? What do the parties want? For what are they willing to commit and strive?

Let's say that a desire is birthed for resolution and restored trust, where forgiveness is chosen as a means of reconciliation or at least the beginning of restoration. In our experience personally and professionally, there may be only one way to start building trust again. If truly desired, trust must once more be granted freely, not because it was or wasn't earned, but simply granted before a trust relationship can be remade, then proven or disproven over time.

> If truly desired, trust must once more be granted freely…

Does it come with risk? Yes. The parties decide and are generally guided first by how much they desire a restored relationship, the degree of real or supposed risk inherent in the effort, and whether or not this kind of restoration is possible without recrimination or selfish intent. It's a tough call but not an impossible one. How much new trust would you and others prefer?

The Value of a Sincere Apology

What does it mean to apologize sincerely for an error you've made? We all make mistakes, so then what?

Consider: how possible is it to genuinely apologize without choosing humility? In my view, no apology can be offered truly from the heart without humility being chosen first.

> No apology can be offered truly from the heart without humility being chosen first.

On the other side, how should you receive a sincere apology from one who has wounded you, overstepped their bounds, or committed an offense? How much openness and humility does this action require? Choosing humility can empower the chooser to receive and accept an apology unconditionally.

An apology is composed of at least two people. One is the person who accepts responsibility for a negative or destructive action, whether intentional or inadvertent, and seeks forgiveness from the offended party, beginning with two powerful words when said with integrity: "I'm sorry." When a person seeks forgiveness while owning his or her responsibility for an action, that person soon realizes that this transaction takes big character and a truly gentle spirit. This person also knows or learns there may be risk involved—that of the other party accepting or rejecting the apology. Often a true apology is followed with, "Will you forgive me?" Humility in action once more.

Once an apology is offered, it is up to the offended party to accept or reject it. If accepted, forgiveness can follow, an account is or can be wiped clean, even if judgment for an offense must be served, and likely a relationship may be restored—a desirable result.

My Awesome Humility and How I Attained It

But what happens when an offended person is offered an apology and does not accept it? Regardless of the reasons for rejection, the matter is not and cannot be completely closed unless both parties agree to close it. Where agreement does not exist, it may be best to simply walk away, forgive the lack of acceptance regardless, and move on.

Someone who hears an apology and refuses it may do so from a self-inflated position of arrogance or revenge. This kind of power positioning actually tends to hurt the offended person more than the offender. No groveling is ever required when an apology is offered sincerely and received humbly! Groveling is not beneficial, wastes time, personhood, energy, and defies dignity.

In a process where restitution may become possible, much is dependent on motive—on both sides. If two sides are adverse in their motives, efforts at restitution may be fruitless.

However, if a chance for restitution or restoration exists, you may choose to act on it for the benefit of all. If you've been offended, strive to be gracious in your dealings with those who have wounded you. Forgiving quickly is superior to becoming bitter and seeking revenge, regardless of the degree of offense. Accepting forgiveness graciously is far better than harboring continued guilt or desires for revenge. If it's done, let it be done.

> Forgiving quickly is superior to becoming bitter and seeking revenge, regardless of the degree of offense. Accepting forgiveness graciously is far better than harboring continued guilt. If it's done, let it be done.

Becoming better is possible when tendencies to become bitter are replaced with forgiveness, forbearance, and love. These are powerful choices, but they are choices. They don't happen by themselves, or apart from exercising humility and desire and then acting on what is truly desired. It takes a secure, maturing, and healthy person to acknowledge someone who admits wrongdoing, offers an apology, and then seeks to receive your forgiveness, and even ask for it.

Forgiveness can also be granted apart from restitution. When it occurs, the offense is no longer held to an account, and a slate is wiped clean. Some people choose to forgive someone who cannot hear them—a deceased person, a person unreachable or unable to receive forgiveness for whatever reason. Freedom reigns or can reign when the bondage of offense is broken by one who no longer desires to live in bitterness or recrimination and chooses to forgive.

Forgiveness does not automatically include forgetting. It seldom does. An offense occurred. Memories may be long and feel overwhelming. What to do with sad and offensive memories, how one allows them to affect life and health, becomes an objective of love of yourself and love for others, in that order, based on the forgiveness model of God.

My Awesome Humility and How I Attained It

Forgetting may not and perhaps cannot be the primary goal when a process of apology is considered. Replace the hard memory with the option to help another from your storehouse of love. You have to choose this action.

Harboring or planning revenge usually does no one any good. If you seethe with revenge, you cannot show mercy. The two cannot coexist in the same heart and mind. You've heard it before: "What goes around comes around." If you treasure ill will, then mercy and forgiveness may not be offered to you when you need it the most and even request it.

When offenses occur, and they will, a true apology can become the first step toward appropriate restitution. Here's the good news: reconciliation can become possible when an offended person doesn't value bitterness more than the desire for grace and healing.

> Reconciliation can become possible when an offended person doesn't value bitterness more than the desire for grace and healing.

If you are the offender, what is your responsibility when you want to make things right? If you are the offended one, what will you do with a sincere apology originating from the heart of the person who wounded you? What should your response be when an offer of restitution is humbly expressed from the person who has offended you?

The Mentors in Your Life

You may not wish to endeavor alone to try to engage in personal self-improvement, behavioral alterations, and the restoration of relationships. Generally, people who want to become better benefit greatly by inviting and then allowing more experienced, mature, and loving people to guide and mentor them in the processes. For many, inviting or including these people as parts of the mix of growth are great options.

I seek to associate with people who have a track record of personal and professional successes and who treat other people well. I want to rub shoulders with, and be influenced by people who possess proven reliability in relationship and function.

Someone has said, "If you want to shoot a moose, go to where the moose are. They generally don't come to you." If you want to get to know people who think positive, whose actions verify an uplifting core character, who are successful, who are "where you want to be," seek them out.

At first, because they may not know you enough to reach out to you, you may have to make initial and diligent efforts to find them. Get to know people like this where possible, and then, if appropriate, ask them to teach and mentor you.

My Awesome Humility and How I Attained It

You have to humble yourself to learn from others more qualified than you. Can you do it?

> You have to humble yourself to learn from others more qualified than you. Can you do it?

Many people have come to me with ambitious career plans, seeking my opinion, or wanting me to hear their goals. My response, after listening, often begins with a question or two, or more: "Who have you interviewed regarding this career? Who in your field of interest is or may already be where you think you want to be? How are they doing? What are their likes and dislikes? What has gone well, what has not, and what do they think they still need to learn? What are their achievements and disappointments, and what truths can you glean from these people?"

How many people have not even considered asking these questions of career professionals?

Seek the input of at least two professionals in your chosen field of interest. Be hungry for knowledge. Be respectful. Take notes. Compare findings.

> Seek the input of at least two professionals in your chosen field of interest. Be hungry for knowledge. Be respectful. Take notes. Compare findings.

Ask, listen, and learn. Professionals who understand your desires for growth likely will grant you their counsel; but you have to humbly and sincerely request. If they don't want to help you, or cannot give you their time and information, move to the next person who will. Be gracious and tenacious at the same time.

> Ask, listen, and learn. Be gracious and tenacious at the same time.

As you engage with these people, evaluate what they say. Ask yourself, "To what degree do I still want to pursue this path?" "How willing am I to stay the course after what I have learned and experienced?"

Not too long after college I eagerly sought the friendship, advice, and counsel of an older gentleman (he was "older" to me ... I was still in my twenties, he in his fifties). He graciously offered his time—a lot of it. He listened and counseled, and as he did he deeply impacted my life. It was a pivotal period. I had just taken my first fulltime job and was responsible for providing weekly programming (music, media, drama, and technical services) for a large organization, working with and supervising upwards of at least 200 individuals depending on the nature of the programs, to audiences numbering 3,000 or more each week.

I was young, clearly not prepared for that kind of responsibility, even though I tried.

My Awesome Humility and How I Attained It

Vern became one of my dearest friends. He was immensely successful, having sold his business, and he had retired around age 50. He began investing in real estate and went on to volunteer his services to non-profits because he wanted to, and he could.

We shared likes, dislikes, music (a lot of it), administration, laughter, and goal-setting. He encouraged, taught, and occasionally confronted. Learning from a wiser and more mature, well-seasoned, sensitive, "world wise" and anchored gentleman, was a smart choice. Vern helped me greatly. I was grateful then, and remain grateful now. He's been gone for many years, but his investments live.

Not all of his counsel was perfect, of course, but he offered me educated and honest perspectives in what often included disheartening times of challenge, personal growth, and stretching. Listening was essential. Learning was more so. Application was required.

> Listening was essential. Learning was more so.
> Application was required.

Do you know how hard it is to talk and listen intently at the same time? Here's an encouragement: listen closely when someone wiser than you is speaking. Learn their truths and then activate them in your own life to the degrees possible.

Several years later another successful business leader became a mentor because I wanted to learn and asked him to teach me. He had actually been an employer of mine in that he had served on a board of directors of an organization for which I worked. At that time he already was the owner of a very large national company. He was humble, gentle, kind, and firm when he needed to be. He was a gifted leader who spoke personal truth and demonstrated high moral character qualities. These deeply endeared him to customers and staff.

I learned much from Chuck. Seeing his operation up close showed me his true character. His treatment of his staff in his large manufacturing firm was exemplary.

There is a truth here I will unpack. It is this: when any leader earns a position of success but poorly manages staff, does not treat them with fairness, respect, or courtesy (a common combination, unfortunately), that is not the kind of leader you may wish to follow.

Great leaders for life and legacy invest in their staff first. Then their customers become the beneficiaries of that investment. Remember that.

> Great leaders for life and legacy invest in their staff first. Then their customers become the beneficiaries of that investment. Remember that.

My Awesome Humility and How I Attained It

If you are the leader, your staff should come first. They, in turn, will acquire and serve your customers. They will adopt similar treatments with which they have been treated — it's the Golden Rule, extended. In building legacy, this model is passed on from company to customer. It works. When a leader sets that kind of tone, and practices true honor and humility the benefits often grow far beyond those who initially receive positive treatment.

Chuck made a huge mark on me. Now deceased, his legacy continues and it still reaches thousands through company employees, customers, and associates. I am one.

A secure individual not only does not mind sharing his or her secrets of success; he or she is eager to teach those who express a genuine desire to learn and grow. Mature and secure people who want to help others grow on their journeys are pleased and in no way threatened by another's success. In fact, he or she celebrates with those who make positive strides.

> Mature and secure people who want to help others grow on their journeys are pleased and in no way threatened by another's success. In fact, he or she celebrates with those who make positive strides.

Completing or Competing?

Let me invite you to think about completing versus competing. The differences between them are distinct, yet they can cooperate and often do when secure individuals set the tone of an engagement.

Completing others is what secure individuals do while striving for their own personal excellence, to be the best they can be. Can or should competing with another person or organization be part of the mix? Perhaps, if needs be, and it often is. There is nothing wrong with business, personal, sports, and other kinds of competition as long as true respect is part of the environment. Secure individuals are interested far more in developing and showcasing positive character than just winning a numbers game.

> Completing others is what secure individuals do while striving for their own personal excellence, to be the best they can be.

> There is nothing wrong with business, personal, sports, and other kinds of competition as long as true respect is part of the environment.

My Awesome Humility and How I Attained It

Yet, secure and balanced persons are interested in winning, too. Let's say you are one of them. When you win, graciously accept the praise and accolades offered to you. Refusing someone else's overtures of adulation where deserved can stymie growth and discourage one who genuinely wants to praise you for your efforts for a job well done.

I believe in winning and working hard. I've done both successfully. I've also tried, worked very hard, and failed. I've learned from these experiences because I wanted to.

What is your take on winning versus losing? How do you handle each?

I believe in supporting and encouraging people who set big goals: those who create and actualize a transferable example of life and legacy for others to observe and follow because they see the benefits, and soar above distasteful distractions, destructive behaviors, or endeavors of competition alone where the goal may be nothing more than winning at a competitor's expense. You know, elevating you so someone else fails then gloating over your supposed superiority.

There's more to life than winning only. Learn this. Certainly become the best you can be in whatever you strive to do. When you win, you should be rewarded. Not everyone should or will receive a first place trophy. Only one can be #1. This is right.

> There's more to life than winning only. Learn this.

What to do with winning: when you win, take more than a victory lap as you relish people's congratulations, though important. Invest in others, and if they'll let you, turn your win into a win for them, whether or not they've performed and competed against you.

Take the higher road. Winning elevates your responsibility to live graciously, invest in, and encourage others.

Learn from winning *and* losing. Grow and grow up.

> Winning elevates your responsibility to live graciously, invest in, and encourage others. Learn from winning *and* losing. Grow and grow up.

How much do you complete versus compete? How possible is it to do both at the same time because both can be right?

Chapter Seven

Slow Down Enough to Do Something Beneficial for You

When is the last time you stopped work and did something designed to benefit you, an activity you truly enjoyed? When is the last time you truly took a "day off" and rested? When is the last time you understood that rest for you, time off and away from the regular grind, is necessary to achieve balance and wellbeing?

Vacations did not last very long in my family when I was a young boy — they occurred about once yearly, and lasted for up to three days. My father and mother were part of a generation who had survived the Great Depression, so learning how to make do and "prepare for a rainy day" was deeply ingrained in the psyche and actions of these two precious people.

Taking lengthy vacations where profitability might be suspended for a time, even for rest, was not considered prudent. Fun was not nearly as important as preparation for what may be experienced on the morrow.

What was lacking for them, through a perspective of generations of backbreaking work and financial hardship, in comparison to a lifestyle of leisure, or one that provided moments of leisure, was balance.

What is balance? In its simplest form it means that no one thing becomes more important than every other thing, and we learn the beauty of engaging in varied activities that have similar weight or importance, not stressing over any, doing all in moderation. Balance, if we desire it, says that we must rest, or die not rested.

You may be gratified to know that when my kids were growing up, we took many more vacations. Treasured photos and memories for sure! But the overall lesson was still being learned.

How much balance do you possess in your life, especially as it relates to not allowing one activity to overshadow all others to the detriment of some?

> How much balance do you possess in your life, especially as it relates to not allowing one activity to overshadow all others to the detriment of some?

How important is a day of rest?

My Awesome Humility and How I Attained It

From Exodus 20:8-10, part of the Ten Commandments (KJV):

> 8 Remember the sabbath day, to keep it holy.
> 9 Six days shalt thou labor, and do all thy work:
> 10 But the seventh day is the sabbath of the LORD thy God: in it thou shalt not do any work, thou, nor thy son, nor thy daughter, thy manservant, nor thy maidservant, nor thy cattle, nor thy stranger that is within thy gates:

For years it was hard for me to take "a day off." Not impossible, but hard. Likely this trait was an inherited conclusion from my upbringing and experience. I also worked for myself, but had numerous clients, "employers" for whom I provided continuous service. My conclusions were that "days off" were not as important as provision for those who hired me. I was wrong.

My son reminded me several months ago of just how important taking a Sabbath day is. My son is right.

Now I take a Sabbath, or day of rest, every week.

It has become vital.

How often do you relax, and as part of your life experience, do something *just for you* which may include observing a recurring day of rest and enjoying times of leisure just because these options are good for you?

Achieving balance likely requires stopping your work, taking time to unwind, and doing something just for you. Relaxation may not initially be seen as beneficial if resting has been rare. Friends have observed, correctly I think, that much depends on a person's priorities: what's important and why. How much does your lifestyle allow you to enjoy a break?

> How much does your lifestyle allow you to enjoy a break?

Friends have stated, again accurately, that it takes true love of you to provide a day of rest for you. Resting regularly is simply a part of the way we are "wired." Setting aside times to regroup, refocus on belief and relief, are intentional because they need to be. Benefits come. They follow the discipline of taking "time off." This is something you do for you because you care about you.

> It takes true love of you to provide a day of rest for you.

One of my high calling life-interests is music production. You may have learned this from the websites. Music is simply a part of who I am. The field of music can be pure joy and extremely hard work. It needs balance.

My Awesome Humility and How I Attained It

A person with two strong sides, I greatly desire to achieve balance between them. It takes dedicated effort to do this … achieving balance doesn't just happen on its own.

My two strong sides are administration (driven, goal-oriented accomplishment) and relationships (taking time for me and others in my life). They are a blessing when in balance. When out of balance, life can look like this:

1. I get a lot done and relationships with others may suffer, or my love of me is not prioritized correctly.

2. I spend so much time and energy relating to others or treasuring me that little or no work gets done.

The music field provides a good study in both of my strong sides and the need to achieve balance. I am grateful to keep learning this.

Actually, sometimes the only way I can know where to concentrate my energies in music, consulting, publishing, or otherwise, is to slow down and take the necessary time to observe the larger picture, and then make more informed choices of where to invest my efforts.

Balance comes in understanding and changing behavior. I've discovered that slowing down a bit allows me to learn and appreciate more, listen intentionally, and speak clearer.

> Balance comes in understanding and changing behavior.

I am still a learner, for sure. Practicing the discipline of slowing down has broadened my perspectives, opened my eyes, and helped me balance life and love. This is good.

Be Still. Know. Appreciate. Love. Enjoy. Celebrate. Work Hard. Play Hard. Sleep Well. Relax!

> Be Still. Know. Appreciate. Love. Enjoy. Celebrate. Work Hard. Play Hard. Sleep Well. Relax!

All of these in combination work to help weaknesses become strengths, and meekness (controlled strength) to be meted out in correct portions for my good and the good of those who receive from me.

Chapter Eight

You Become a Leader When You Care More about Others than Yourself, Because You Are Secure in Who You Are

The journey of becoming your own person because you treasure yourself, and then become secure enough to help others out of your "wealth of health" is a lifelong endeavor. It probably doesn't happen overnight (although I suppose it could). Like any journey, this one features ups, downs, twists, turns, straight paths, and dangerous bends in the road.

The story is told of a wealthy, elderly woman who wished to hire a driver. Her age was preventing her efforts to maneuver her car well, especially up and through the mountains in her surrounding area, so she sought to engage a younger person who could shuttle her around safely.

Several candidates applied for the job. She told each one, "I want to see how close to the edge of the cliffs you can come." Each drove the course. Each made the trip successfully.

The young man who obtained the position was the one who had driven her car as far away from the edge of the cliffs as possible. When asked why he had done this, he replied, "Because my cargo is more valuable than my daring."

Weighing conditions and confronting difficult turns require knowledge, judgment, and wisdom. Knowledge (knowing what is right) and judgment (evaluating perspectives) are products of wisdom (sufficient understanding to choose well), and wisdom is a gift. Whether or not you are a praying person, you may wish to humble yourself and pray for wisdom, and then slow down enough to allow wisdom to take root in your heart and soul. Praying for wisdom and then allowing it to become activated within you is a good choice.

> Praying for wisdom and then allowing it to become activated within you is a good choice.

Wisdom calls for you to choose a positive self-image. Developing a positive self-image is a proper and beneficial goal. If the reasons you desire a new or renewed self-image are rooted in a balanced and expanded desire to help and encourage others, you have prioritized correctly. You are in a better position to "Love your neighbor as yourself."

My Awesome Humility and How I Attained It

Many people truly believe they have failed. Perhaps they have. Perhaps you are one of them. The question may not be whether failure has accompanied you; rather, whether you have learned from those times when failure was your portion.

In many consulting engagements I have asked this question of groups: "How do you learn? What are the preferred ways of learning for you?" Without skipping a beat the first answer usually offered is this: "By my mistakes and through failures." Fair enough. Mistakes and failures can provide powerful teaching moments.

Conversely, how often do you allow yourself to learn from your victories? It is vital you learn from *both* failures and successes.

Believing that you will fail may be a sure sign of insecurity tightening its grip around you, allowing it to control you. Your choice, and it is your choice, is to counteract failure or its tendencies with new and renewed, positive attitudes and actions. Nothing and no one controls you unless you allow them to. Into what kinds of images of yourself do you allow negativity to invade and conquer?

Replace negativity with optimism and hard work. Rebalance your priorities. Seek to love and be loved. Remember: you are not a failure unless you choose to be one. Since you are not a failure, stop acting like one.

What behaviors of yours tend to showcase a lack of self-image, confidence, and self-worth? What better behaviors would you like to substitute for these?

What activities would you like to choose which would bolster more positive outlooks and encourage you?

You are invited to write them down and change your behavior. You are in charge of you if you want to be.

> You are in charge of you if you want to be.

Probably one of the greatest speeches in the English language is Lincoln's Second Inaugural Address, delivered on March 4, 1865. This speech concludes with these words:

> *"With malice toward none, with charity for all, with firmness in the right as God gives us to see the right, let us strive on to finish the work we are in, to bind up the nation's wounds, to care for him who shall have borne the battle and for his widow and his orphan, to do all which may achieve and cherish a just and lasting peace among ourselves and with all nations."*

Here is that quote again, interspersed with interpretation. See how these lofty ideals and ideas are connected to positive attitudes, choices, and decisive actions:

My Awesome Humility and How I Attained It

"With malice toward none, with charity toward all **(attitudes and choices)** *let us strive to finish the work we are in, to bind up the nation's wounds, to care for him who shall have borne the battle and for his widow and his orphan, to do all which may achieve and cherish a just and lasting peace among ourselves and with all nations* **(actions)***."*

Be tenacious about doing what is right to the best of your understanding of what right is.

Your beliefs become your causes. Your priorities become your plans. Your plans become your actions. Your actions make a mark on you and affect those around you.

> Your beliefs become your causes. Your priorities become your plans. Your plans become your actions.
> Your actions make a mark on you and affect those around you.

Consider these questions and your answers to them:

1. What are your primary beliefs and upon what do you base them?

2. About what causes are you passionate and to which do you dedicate your efforts?

3. What priorities move you and help you inspire others?

4. What well-thought-out plans become your guideposts for action and help you to change your behaviors for the better?

5. What actions will you choose to produce positive changes in you, and when will you begin to choose them and act upon them?

6. How can you be assured that your actions are meritorious?

7. What actions of yours will others see and become better for this observance and inspired to emulate you?

You lead others when your actions become models of good behavior you wish to duplicate into other people's lives. These are people into whom you invest lovingly because you love yourself first.

> You lead others when your actions become models of good behavior you wish to duplicate into other people's lives. These are people into whom you invest lovingly because you love yourself first.

My Awesome Humility and How I Attained It

People who see you may desire to learn from you because they like and appreciate what you show them. When you teach them, you do so because you love yourself first and seek to invest and share that love into others. You can become a positive example of effective and long-lasting leadership and mentoring if you so desire.

> You can become a positive example of effective and long-lasting leadership and mentoring if you so desire.

But this process begins in integrity only when your love priorities — you first, then others — are present and active. In fact, I would go so far as to state that only a person who truly loves himself or herself is in the best position to lead because they have become aware of how blessed they truly are, and they want to share those blessings.

Only secure people, who are learning to love themselves because they desire security (self-assurance) and continually work to personally improve, can love others fully and selflessly lead them to love in the process.

One who does not love himself or herself, or loves less than he or she should, can be prevented, by their own estimation of themselves, from helping and encouraging others.

Within a loving individual, ambition takes a rightful place in the core of character. When ambition is balanced with selfless giving, a leader can be born.

"No one accomplishes anything of merit by wishing and dreaming alone. Action and hard work, born of a steadfast desire to succeed and overcome obstacles must accompany desire, hope, aspiration, and dependence on God; for then only will achievements come."
~ From the book *Lincoln – The Making of a Leader*

> Within a loving individual, ambition takes a rightful place in the core of character. When ambition is balanced with selfless giving, a leader can be born.

Personal achievements are not won in isolation; they are born from the investments of others who invest in you because you desire growth, and they emerge from others into whom you invest out of your storehouse of love and security.

Balance what you desire and what you seek to share. That is what true love does.

> Balance what you desire and what you seek to share. That is what true love does.

Chapter Nine

Be Well, Love Well, Lead Well, Invest Well, and Feel Good about It

You are a gift. You are a treasure. You are special in the sight of God. Believe this and rest on this truth.

Consider the impediments to growth of the real you. If you are fearful, what is the source of that fear? Failure, repression, recrimination, cruelty (regardless of source), criticism, being told you are not worth it? If fear is present, that condition may tempt you to cover your insecurity with arrogance or intimidation. If you don't want fear, don't let it in. Refuse fear. You are bigger than that. Replace it with love and love others as you love yourself.

Arrogance cancels humility and substitutes dominance for love when it is allowed to rule you or control you. Remember that you are in the best position to help another when you are humble enough to recognize that you, too, may have needed assistance and were not too proud to ask for it, and that you have graciously accepted it when it came. Don't let fear, arrogance, feelings of "I'm not worth it," other people's negative opinions, or savage and unsubstantiated backstabbing and false accusations behind or about you, or your own personal stubbornness and defensiveness, rule you.

Rise and soar above these negative conditions, and say, "No!" to the temptations to get sucked into the cesspool of self-deprecation. Only you can do this for you. You must believe in you and then humble you. You rise up because you truly want to, not because you dwell in feelings of pervasive guilt or a lack of self-worth.

Do not accept living and wallowing in insecurity. The choice you make to not follow the path of substituting the priceless person you are with inferior feelings of small worth, is a choice you make. No one else makes it for you. You make it for yourself. You can choose better if you want to.

Protect yourself when needed, preserve your dignity. Then give yourself away. It is possible to not be selfish when you cognitively replace selfishness with desires to serve and perform the actions that prove it, not requesting or requiring credit for your deeds. Your own self is vital. Remember this and then exercise control of you as you strive to help others.

My Awesome Humility and How I Attained It

> Your own self is vital. Remember this and then exercise control of you as you strive to help others.

That choice may not be easy, but it is possible. If you are a person who believes in God and seeks to live in faith, pray and ask God for help, then accept the help when it comes. No excuses. Don't deny for yourself what God wants to give you.

"Be well!" is a phrase born of good and sincere wishes when expressed sincerely. Its origin does not include fear of failure or groveling in mistakes. In its truest form, "Be well!" is a genuine blessing. Do you know how blessed you really are?

One of the exercises that may help you is to physically write down as many things as possible for which you are heart-grateful. Then take that list and offer it to God in thanksgiving. Post it so you can see it often. Thankfulness is a precursor of becoming whole in mind and spirit. It is impossible to be destructively critical of yourself or others when you truly possess a thankful heart.

Remember: loving another is possible only when you love yourself. Also remember: you can't give away something you do not have. The characteristics of those who care are traits of those who lead well and help others for the right reasons. This process begins with balanced self-love.

We see evidence of transferable and selfless love in meritorious leaders who impact, influence, and invest in others. True leadership is leadership that serves more than it demands and helps more than it hinders. This leadership is born of and borne on selfless love.

Leadership that only takes and doesn't give, illustrates greed and is marked with insecurity. That kind of leadership is not practiced by someone who wants to lead well for life and legacy. Investment in others for their benefit costs a true leader what he or she can pay, and he or she is happy to grant what is possible for the benefit of a follower.

> True leadership is leadership that serves more than it demands and helps more than it hinders. This leadership is born of and borne on selfless love.

Feel good about you, not from a position of self-aggrandizement; rather, from a position of controlled strength and genuine humility. Don't brag and talk about you. Let others do that, and accept praise and accolades with genuine thanks. True thanksgiving first receives praise graciously when offered, and then hands it back to the giver without boasting about the exchange. Can you do this?

The opportunities to be well, love well, lead well, invest well, and feel good about it, come daily. Many of these opportunities you may create for yourself. Good for you. You've heard it: "If you want friends, show yourself

My Awesome Humility and How I Attained It

friendly." Same truths: "If you want to be loved, love. If you want to be well, encourage others in their quests to become whole. If you want happiness, strive to make others happy."

Well-placed humor is a technique I often choose in helping others win. It helps me win, too. Humor can take many forms. Develop enough security to laugh at yourself, not at the expense of others! A person who uses humor to grow personally, to illustrate a point and then can laugh at himself or herself is one who is endeavoring to exercise balance, and generally becomes better for it.

Replace greed and self-promoting desires to elevate yourself at the expense of others, with giving and helping others succeed. If insecurity causes you to stumble as you try, you can rise above this. You can soar like an eagle on the wings of God-given controlled strength and grace. Be grateful and giving.

Understand, if faithfulness from others is what you want, choose faithfulness for the real you — first in your attitudes and actions toward yourself and then in your contributions to and with others. Exercise authentic consistency, follow through, become trustworthy, extend trust, practice genuine courtesy, and then offer a helping hand.

Substitute negatives with positives. It's a worthwhile exchange and one you must do because you want to, not because you are made to.

What kinds of living experiences do you want, and for what purpose? Focus your mind on benefiting others because you treasure you. This can be a winning combination of motives and methods. This can become your lifestyle, a transferable model, an example of controlled strength and humility.

> Focus your mind on benefiting others because you treasure you.

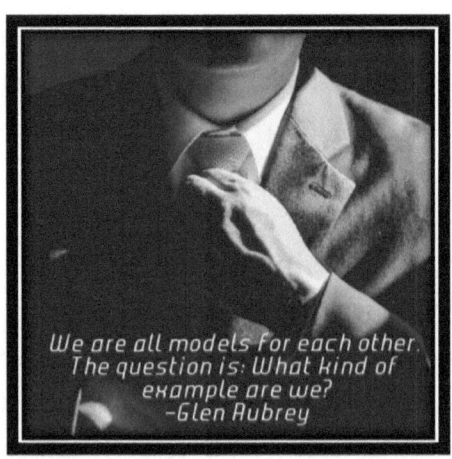

Chapter Ten

It's Work and You Are Worth It

The Bible records the teachings of Jesus, as you've likely heard. One of the most powerful instructions, known and recognized by many, is this one found in the Gospel of Luke, Chapter 6, and verse 31:

"Do to others as you would have them do to you."

How would you like others to treat you? It's clear from this scripture that you can set the tone and many of the parameters of healthy engagement. If you treat others poorly, expect the same. Conversely, if you treat others well, anticipate better results.

You stand a much greater opportunity of treating others well when you value or love yourself, first. How strongly do you believe this?

You must convince yourself of your worth. A process of convincing may sound difficult to accomplish, but it is possible. Self-doubt, questioning your motives and methods, and dwelling in insecurities may interrupt your progress and seek to negatively influence your thinking. Expect this.

Rise above the negativity. It's a choice. Soar above the myriad of excuses that can permeate your thoughts and, if allowed, thwart you in a genuine desire to improve and become a blessing to others.

Naysayers are not worth your time and energy, nor are dishonest connivers, backstabbers, liars, and thieves. Nor are overtly critical people who seek to destroy you and others. Nor are people whose main desires are to put you and others down in their perverted quests to elevate themselves. Nor are self-absorbed people bent on destruction of you, your principles and practices, and the positive character attributes they refuse for themselves and try to inhibit or destroy in others.

The best ways to deal with negative people are to shower them with positivity and love. Treat them as you want to be treated. They may reject you, leave you alone, or even become better. Whatever you do, don't try to convince them of your positive outlooks. Listening is hard if not impossible for insecure and negative people. They often don't want advice, truth, counsel, or overtures of peace, and generally shun solid friendships, too. They make their own circumstances. Do not enter their domains. Become an example of confident assurance, the opposite of destructive insecurity. Then help them if they genuinely seek help. Be kind because God and other people have been kind to you.

Become the master of your own domain in submission to God. Love Him first. Then love you. Show to others what you would like them to eventually present to themselves and to you and others. It is a transferable model.

> Become the master of your own domain in submission to God.

Developing a positive self-image is work and you are worth the effort. The more convinced you become of your value, the more controlled strength and genuine humility you'll choose.

During 2018, a friend casually shared a phrase in a text. It was "rested and home." It hit me profoundly.

<u>Rested</u> is more than being "on break," "at ease," "content," or "relaxed," though the term can include these. But it's more.

<u>Home</u> may be a physical dwelling, though home is not necessarily defined by a place. Home, in this sense, is "where the heart is."

> "Home is where the heart is,
> To be content where faith is strong.
> Home is where our values are,
> Where there's time to pray, to rest, and to belong."
> ~ From the song, "Take Us Home" Words and music by Glen Aubrey © 1993. All Rights Reserved.

What is "home" to you? Home may be a condition where life is simpler and welcoming to you and others. It's a stress-free environment, a place of peace.

Living a simpler life ... 'sounds good, doesn't it? A simpler life is composed of positive attributes and attitudes for one who is secure and enjoys personal love for the right reasons.

"A simpler life" may have several meanings. One definition may be: a lifestyle uncluttered by distracting trends, unending tasks, testy people, relentless toils, dire temptations, and unruly tempests of negativity that can confront and hinder personal growth.

What separates you from the important balance of faith, family, rest, and work? It is not possible, nor profitable to try to isolate yourself from the familiar forces you may face, good and bad. Living in health means possessing the strength and desire to deal with whatever comes along in right and balanced ways.

My Awesome Humility and How I Attained It

Where excesses and negative influences place undue and destructive pressures on you, you may choose to seek and work toward what you would define as a simpler life. This may be a place where you can freely grow, be "at home and at rest," enjoying peace, not continually confronting pieces of toxic negativity that try to drag you down.

How can you live with yourself, rested and home, and at peace? How can you live without the burdensome shackles that bind you to a life of smallness or feelings of unworthiness, failure, and hopelessness?

Chains forged by yourself or others can be broken. It's what forgiveness and restitution are all about. Some chains are strong and mighty, true, but forgiveness, love, and a desire to live free can be stronger than these confinements.

It may be beneficial for you to seek professional counsel, the wisdom and experience of others you trust, those who have shown you stability and balance, to help you learn better how to live free, enjoy yourself more, and become a person who can help others out of your controlled strength, humility, and confidence. Trusted clergy, close friends, counselors, people who will listen without judging, those who may offer wise counsel, may be exactly what's right for you when you need help.

Glen Aubrey

In 2018 I composed a song, based on the phrase, "Rested and Home." At first, the piece was only music, no lyrics. Over several weeks, lyrics were created.

I share this song with you to encourage you. You will observe attributes that belong to a person and position of faith. Are you an individual who trusts, desires, and endeavors to grow in a positive relationship with God and others? Perhaps these words will become meaningful to you.

Rested and Home

© 2018 Glen Aubrey. All Rights Reserved.

Rested and Home from the work of the day,
All thanks to God, He has blessed our way.
His love assures, His strength secures,
From stress released, dwelling in peace,
Rested, Home.

Love enters here, soothes the heart, dries the tear,
Comforts the soul, making wounded whole.
In love embraced, warmed by His grace,
Drawn to His side, in Him abide,
Rested, Home.

Calling to me, "Come away, be refreshed,
Strong in My power, you will face each test."
Living His plan, kept by His hand,
God's presence near, love conquers fear,
Rested, Home.

My Awesome Humility and How I Attained It

Healing my heart, and renewing my mind,
His love surrounds, peaceful, gentle, kind.
I choose His will, following still,
Serving my Lord, in Him restored,
Rested, Home.

Closing Thoughts

The conclusion of the book, *Lincoln – The Making of a Leader,* written in 2017, is applicable here. "The more I've learned, the more I want to learn. Perhaps you are one of these people with an insatiable desire for knowledge. Knowing truths is the beginning, of course; but applying them — creating action steps because of your desire to change your behavior for the better — must follow if learning is to become living.

"Hopefully you and I have shared truths in this book which you may find helpful. What changes do you desire to make so that what you've learned becomes new action within your life? I wish you well on your journey."

Your desire to love you so you can benefit others is a noble, right, and just cause. Achieving worthwhile causes takes effort. Your desires come first and diligent work follows.

Chosen humility becomes a blessed byproduct of your love of yourself and others. Growing in this balance is a good goal. Exercise faith in God and love Him first. Then love yourself as you love others. Engage in wholesome interactions with others who share likeminded beliefs.

Credits in Order of Appearance

Social media campaign: Jenafer Aubrey

Website design: Randy Beck, My Domain Tools,
www.mydomaintools.com

Imagery: www.dreamstime.com/free-photos
Copyright © 2000-2018 Dreamstime. All rights reserved.
Public Domain Images Licensed
Under the Creative Commons Zero (CC0) License

https://creativecommons.org/publicdomain/zero/1.0/

https://www.history.com/topics/american-revolution/declaration-of-independence
Public Domain

The Holy Bible, King James Authorized Version, 1611 (KJV)
Public Domain

Credits in Order of Appearance

The Holy Bible, New International Version® (NIV) ® Copyright
©1973, 1978, 1984, 2011 by Biblica, Inc. ®
Used by permission. All rights reserved worldwide.

Excerpts from
Leadership Is – How to Build Your Legacy –
A Business Life Investment Model
By Glen Aubrey © 2012
Creative Team Publishing, San Diego, California
Used by permission.

"Keep the Dream Alive"
Words and Music by Glen Aubrey
© 2009 Glen Aubrey. All Rights Reserved.
Used by permission of Creative Music Enterprises,
Glen Aubrey www.CreativeMusicEnterprises.com
Creative Team Publishing, San Diego, California

Policing Peace – What America Can Do Now To
Avoid Future Tragedies. © 2017 By Larry Wolf
Creative Team Publishing, Ft. Worth, Texas
www.policingpeace.com
Quotations from this book are used by permission.

Reference to Taylor (last name withheld by request) is used with permission of Taylor.

Credits in Order of Appearance

Quote from Lincoln's Second Inaugural Address is in the Public Domain.

Quotes from *Lincoln – The Making of a Leader* © 2017 are used by permission of Creative Team Publishing.

Excerpts from the lyrics to the song, "Take Us Home"
Words and Music by Glen Aubrey © 1993 Glen Aubrey.
All Rights Reserved.
Used by permission.

"Rested and Home"
Words and Music Glen Aubrey
© 2018 Glen Aubrey. All Rights Reserved.
Used by permission of Creative Music Enterprises,
Glen Aubrey www.CreativeMusicEnterprises.com
Creative Team Publishing, Ft. Worth, Texas

*****

Products and Services

You are invited to contact Glen Aubrey and his teams for products and services.

www.glenaubrey.com

<u>Book Publishing</u>
Creative Team Publishing (CTP)
If you are an author: "We Want to Publish Your Creation!"
www.CreativeTeamPublishing.com

<u>Music Performance, Production, Promotion, Publishing</u>
Creative Music Enterprises (CME)
www.creativemusicenterprises.com

<u>Conferences, Consultation, and Coaching</u>
Creative Team Resources Group (CTRG)
Building Relationships. Making More.™
www.ctrg.com

<u>Non-Profit Organization</u>
<u>Conferences, Consultation, and Coaching</u>
Creative Ministry Teams (CMT)
www.creativeministryteams.org

*****

About the Author

I enjoy traveling, especially to Gettysburg, Washington, D.C., Europe, and the Middle East. I treasure multi-cultural experiences and am fulfilled when conducting conference center presentations and speaking engagements. Enjoyments in life include walking, bicycle riding, and being with family and close friends; also a fireplace, my dogs, listening to classical music and profound artistic works. I appreciate, compose, and arrange multiple styles of music. I earnestly engage in creatively stimulating conversations on uplifting topics, listening and responding to other people's well-thought-out perspectives. I love to laugh. I thoroughly enjoy good football and baseball games. I am a student and teacher, a follower and leader.

Further, "I acknowledge that I have a long way to go in learning what life is all about. I acknowledge that I am willing to work hard to achieve what I believe I am called to do. I also willingly and joyfully acknowledge dependence on God."
~ From *Lincoln – The Making of a Leader*

~ Glen Aubrey, August, 2018

www.ingramcontent.com/pod-product-compliance
Lightning Source LLC
Chambersburg PA
CBHW030449010526
44118CB00011B/856